A LITTLE HISTORY
OF
SCOTLAND

by Heather Morris

Design & cover by Peter Lawson

Brown Dog Books
Bath

First published in the UK in 2006 by
Brown Dog Books
Bath BA2 3LR
All rights reserved

Produced in the UK
Printed in Malta

Reprinted in 2007 (twice)

ISBN: 1 903 056 241

Contents

A Brief History of Scotland

A Brief History of Scotland

Timeline of Scottish history

4000BC	Earliest surviving buildings
80	Roman Julius Agricola advanced across the River Clyde
122	Hadrian's Wall begun
843	Kenneth MacAlpin united the Scots and Picts as one nation
1040	Macbeth killed Duncan and became King
1057	Malcolm III killed Macbeth and became King
1107	Alexander I became King of Scots, but David I was King in Lothian and Strathclyde breaking Scotland into parts again
1124	Alexander died and David became King of all Scotland
1295	The 'Auld Alliance' between Scotland and France was signed
1296	Scotland was conquered by Edward I and the 'Stone of Destiny' was taken to Westminster Abbey
1305	William Wallace was executed
1314	Battle of Bannockburn when Robert the Bruce defeats the English
1320	The Declaration of Arbroath
1411	University of St. Andrews founded
1559	John Knox's sermon at Perth started the Reformation in Scotland
1587	Mary Queen of Scots executed
1603	Union of the Crowns as James VI of Scotland became James I of England
1642	English Civil war spread conflict into Scotland
1692	The massacre of Glencoe
1695	Bank of Scotland founded
1707	Act of Union when Scotland was formally united with England
1715	First Jacobite rebellion when the 'Old Pretender' invaded
1744	The world's first Golf Club was founded in Edinburgh

1745	Bonnie Prince Charlie returned to Scotland and the second Jacobite rebellion began
1746	Battle of Culloden when Jacobites were defeated by the Government troops
1768	The first edition of the Encylopaedia Britannica was published in Edinburgh
1770	The River Clyde became a major thoroughfare for ships
1812	The world's first passenger steamship 'The Comet' was launched
1826	Scotland's first commercial railway was opened between Edinburgh and Dalkeith
1846	Potato crop failed and mass emigration
1870	The first rugby international was played between Scotland and England
1872	Rangers Football Club was founded
1879	Tay Bridge Disaster - over 70 train passengers were killed when the bridge collapsed
1888	Celtic Football Club was founded
1890	Forth Rail Bridge opened
1938	Cunard White Star liner the 'Queen Elizabeth' was launched in Clydebank
1943	German bombing raid killed over 1000 people in Clydebank and Glasgow
1950	Scottish Nationalists stole the 'Stone of Destiny' from Westminster Abbey
1964	Forth Road Bridge, the longest suspension bridge in Europe, was opened
1967	The QE2, the last of the great Clyde-built passenger liners, was launched
1975	The first oil was piped ashore from the North Sea at Peterhead
1996	The 'Stone of Destiny' was returned to Edinburgh Castle from London
1999	A Scottish Parliament was re-instated after 292 years

Early history

Iron Age broch at Dun Carloway

Scotland has some of the most remarkable surviving Neolithic and early Bronze age monuments in the British Isles. This is a vast period of history – from about 4000BC to around 700BC. Neolithic peoples were the first farmers who began clearing woodland and building monuments. In most parts of the UK, domestic buildings were probably constructed of wood and very little remains, but in Orkney (where there was no timber) there is a wonderful stone farmhouse and barn which has been dated back as far as 4000BC, before the Pyramids were built.

The larger village of Skara Brae includes seven or eight one-room stone dwellings. They have stone beds and shelves and recessed cupboards, with a hearth in each hut. Covered passages lead from one dwelling to another. Earth is piled up around to give shelter from the wind. There is even a drain from each of the houses, leading to a common sewer.

More common are the mysterious stone circles and elaborate tombs that these peoples left. There is much new evidence that these constructions formed the focus of village life and people lived in and around them for generations. Charred bones, pottery, stone axes have all been found which suggest a rich and skilled culture.

Again, the Orkneys contain some of the most remarkable examples. The Ring of Brogdar on mainland Orkney is one of the most complete with 27 of the original 67 stones still standing. Nearby are the four Steness stones, the tallest in Scotland.

The Bronze age saw a change in many of the cultural patterns – with individual burials and much more evidence of settled agriculture. Thousands of beautifully wrought bronze weapons, tools, implements and jewellery have been found. By about 500BC there is the first evidence of the Celtic tradition in Scotland and there was much movement of peoples to and from Continental Europe. Again, it is in Scotland that some of the most impressive Iron Age settlements have survived. Known as 'brochs' or 'duns' these were large round stone houses with immensely thick walls that could be as high as 13m. In Shetland these remains are closely linked to good grazing land, again suggesting the importance of agriculture and stock rearing.

Picts and Scots

The first real north/south divide in Britain could be dated back to 100AD. The Romans had invaded the south in 43AD and their original ambition was to occupy the whole of Britain. However, 50 years later, they were admitting defeat in Scotland and Emperor Hadrian began building the wall between Newcastle and Bowness on the west coast in 122AD. The Picts and Scots north of this remained outside Rome's control.

The Picts (the name means 'painted or tattooed' people) and the Scots (originally from Ireland) were direct descendants of the Iron Age groups who had built such formidable monuments in earlier centuries. The Picts dominated the areas north of the Clyde but became increasingly drawn into bloody conflict with Viking invaders and southern Scottish tribes.

One chronicle recounts how a great banquet was held at Scone where the Pictish King and his nobles were plied with drink until they became quite drunk. Then the Scots pulled the bolts from the benches, tipping the Picts into traps dug underneath. The pits were set with sharp blades so the falling Picts were impaled. Trapped and unable to defend themselves, the surviving Picts were murdered and their bodies, clothes and ornaments "plundered."

By the 10th century the Picts have disappeared from history.

First King of Scotland

Kenneth MacAlpin is considered to be the first king of the united Scots and Picts and of Scotland north of a line between the Forth and Clyde rivers. He died in about 858 and by 1034, through inheritance and warfare, the Scots had secured control over Lothian, Cumbria, and Strathclyde - roughly the territory of modern mainland Scotland. The Isles continued to be independent. In 1305 the kingdom was divided into Scotland, Lothian, and Galloway; by the 14th century the whole land was known as Scotland and all its inhabitants were called Scots, whatever their origin.

Kenneth's male descendants provide kings in Scotland for the next two centuries. Their main struggle was to establish Scotland's independence from England.

Looking north across the River Forth

9

Macbeth

King of Scots from 1040-1057, whose life was the basis of Shakespeare's play Macbeth. Many of the characters in the play were based on real people, though Shakespeare took many liberties with history. Macbeth was probably a grandson of King Kenneth II. Macbeth established himself on the throne after killing his cousin King Duncan I in battle near Elgin, (not as in Shakespeare, by murdering Duncan in bed). However, after this unfortunate start his rule was nothing like as bloodthirsty as Shakespeare suggested. Macbeth ruled a largely peaceful kingdom for 17 years.

In 1046 Siward, Earl of Northumbria, unsuccessfully attempted to overthrow Macbeth in favour of Malcolm, eldest son of Duncan I. By 1050 Macbeth felt secure enough to leave Scotland for a pilgrimage to Rome. But in 1054 he was forced by Siward to yield part of southern Scotland to Malcolm. Three years later Macbeth was killed in battle by Malcolm, with assistance from the English.

William Wallace

Statue of William Wallace in Edinburgh Castle

'This is the truth I tell you: of all things freedom's most fine.
Never submit to live, my son, in the bonds of slavery entwined.'
William Wallace - His uncle's proverb, from Bower's
Scotichronicon c.1440s

In 1296 Scotland had been conquered - many of the Scots
nobles were imprisoned, they were harshly taxed and
expected to serve the English King Edward I in his military
campaigns against France. In May 1297 Wallace, the
younger son of a minor Scottish knight, slew the English
Sheriff of Lanark and started a rebellion as men 'oppressed
by the burden of servitude' joined him 'like a swarm of bees'.

On 11th September Wallace achieved a stunning victory at
the Battle of Stirling Bridge. Over 5000 English were slain,
including their despised treasurer, Hugh Cressingham, whose

flayed skin was taken as a trophy of victory and used to make a belt for Wallace's sword. Wallace became Commander of the Scottish army, was knighted and named Guardian of Scotland.

Wallace then took the war into the north of England, raiding around Newcastle and wreaking havoc across the north. But the English army took revenge at Falkirk in 1298 when Edward's Welsh archers rained death on the Scots spearmen. When the French abandoned Scotland, the Scottish leaders saw no hope of victory and capitulated, recognising Edward I as overlord in 1304. Only Wallace refused to submit. He was declared an outlaw and was captured at near Glasgow in August 1305.

Wallace was taken to London for a show trial in Westminster Hall. He was charged with being an outlaw and a traitor. At his trial he had no lawyers, no jury, he wasn't allowed to speak. Inevitably he was found guilty and was immediately dragged by horses four miles through London to Smithfield for execution. There he was hanged but cut down while still alive. Then he was disembowelled and his entrails were thrown upon a fire and, finally, his head was chopped off. His head was set on a pole on London Bridge, and other parts of his body were sent north as a warning to the Scots.

Edward destroyed the man, but strengthened the myth. Wallace became a martyr, the symbol of Scotland's struggle for freedom.

Robert the Bruce

Possibly the most famous of the early Kings of Scotland (1306-29), who freed Scotland from English rule, winning the decisive Battle of Bannockburn in 1314 against Edward III and ultimately confirming Scottish independence in the Treaty of Northampton.

Whether the legend of the spider is true or not Robert the Bruce certainly had a long and difficult struggle. Three of his four brothers were murdered, his wife imprisoned and he himself went into hiding on the island of Rathlin off Ireland. The legend of the spider is said to come from this time as the Bruce watched a spider try and try again to construct a web across the entrance to his cave. He was impressed by the creature's resilience and determination - each time it failed it climbed up again and tried once more. He took a lesson from the spider and tried again....

When the Bruce died his body was buried in Dunfermline Abbey, but his heart was removed and taken by Sir James Douglas on a pilgrimage to the Holy Land. Douglas was killed on the way but, according to tradition, the heart was recovered and brought back to Melrose Abbey.

Mary Queen of Scots

Mary became Queen of Scotland when she was only six days old in December 1542. At the age of five, she was betrothed to the French Dauphin Francis and was sent to be brought up at the French Court. After they married in 1558 Mary became Queen of France as well as Scotland. But Francis died the following year and Mary returned to Scotland.

Although Mary was a Catholic and Scotland was then a Protestant country, at first she ruled successfully. But her marriage in 1565 to Lord Darnley triggered a spiral of disaster. In spring 1566 Darnley burst into her chamber in Holyroodhouse, threatened the pregnant queen and murdered her secretary, David Riccio. Despite the birth of their son James, their relationship did not improve and when Darnley was murdered, suspicion fell on Mary.

Her marriage only three months later to the Earl of Bothwell (believed to be Darnley's murderer) brought her inevitable ruin. Her Protestant Lords forced her to abdicate in favour of her infant son James.

Mary fled to England, believing that Queen Elizabeth I would support her cause, but instead she was held captive in England for 19 years. Mary became the focus of a long series of Catholic plots against Elizabeth, who finally lost patience and ordered her execution. Mary died at Fotheringhay Castle in Northamptonshire on 8 February 1587, at the age of 44.

Union of Crowns 1603

When Elizabeth I died childless, Mary Queen of Scots' son, now James VI of Scotland, became James I of England. He would have liked his two kingdoms to be completely united but Scotland retained its own parliament, Church, laws and educational system.

James enjoyed his life in the English court, and returned to Scotland only once, in 1617. He liked to boast that he now ruled his northern kingdom with a stroke of his pen, but he lost touch with the feelings of the Scottish people.

The early optimism of many Scots nobles also turned to disillusionment. They expected titles and offices but these never materialised and the Scottish kingship and court - the centre of Scottish society and patronage – simply vanished south. With the monarchy gone, the Protestant Church and nobles formed the core of a new Scottish identity.

This conflict came to the fore when James tried to bring the worship and government of the Church of Scotland into line with the Church of England. He met with strong opposition and did not try again to introduce ecclesiastical innovations. He died on 27 March 1625.

Act of Union 1707

The reasons for the Union of the Parliaments (which was unpopular with many Scottish people) were a complex mix of religion, trade and politics. During the English Civil War, many Scots had supported the monarchy and when Charles II died the crown passed to the Catholic James II (James VII of Scotland). He was seen as the legitimate heir to the Stuart line so when he was deposed in favour of the Protestants William and Mary there were uprisings in Scotland in support of James and the Jacobite cause. The Act of Settlement in 1701 preventing a Catholic from becoming monarch, ensured that James' heirs would remain exiled.

In a poorly attended Scottish Parliament the MPs, under intense economic pressure, voted for the Union and on 16th January 1707 the Act of Union was signed. The Scottish parliament was dissolved and England and Scotland became one country. Scotland kept its own legal and religious systems but coinage, taxation, trade, parliaments and flags were united. The red cross of St. George was combined with the blue cross of St. Andrew to create the first union flag.

Jacobite rebellions

When the crown passed to George I, Elector of Hanover, many felt that Britain's interests were being betrayed. It was in Scotland, however, that resistance turned to rebellion as the Highland clans rallied to the cause of the deposed Stuarts. With the support of Louis XIV of France, James Stuart, the 'Old Pretender', attempted a Jacobite uprising. But by the time he landed at Peterhead in 1715, his disorganised supporters had been defeated by the English army.

His son, Bonnie Prince Charlie, did not abandon the cause and his invasion in 1745 was initially more successful. He conquered most of Scotland and brought his army as far south as Derby, only 200k from London. But the expected support did not materialise, he was forced to retreat and his army was destroyed by the Duke of Cumberland's forces at Culloden in 1746. Bonnie Prince Charlie escaped back to France, with help from Flora Macdonald, but his unfortunate followers were not so lucky. This defeat heralded a period of savage repression for the Highland clans.

Their culture was destroyed: it became a hanging offence to speak Gaelic or even to read the Bible; Highlanders were forbidden to carry weapons; anyone wearing the tartan could be imprisoned for six months for a first offence, and on second conviction be transported for seven years. Many of the rich fled the Highlands so that by the end of the 18th century three-fifths of Hebridean landlords were already absentees in London.

Highland clearances

A Highland croft

1792 became known as 'The Year of the Sheep' when Sir John Sinclair introduced the Cheviot sheep to his Langwell estate in Caithness. The Cheviot's large size, its hardiness, tolerance of Highland conditions, and its production of great quantities of high-quality wool and meat meant that sheep-farming suddenly became immensely more profitable. Also, sheep were not a liability to the landlord. Unlike people they were not dependent upon crops and did not seek the support of the laird when crops failed.

It was the death-knell for the traditional way of life for tens of thousands of people across the Highlands and Islands. In Sutherland alone between 1807 and 1821 some 6-10,000 people were evicted, often with great violence, to make way for sheep. Many moved to new settlements on the coast where they struggled to make a living.

Other traditional sources of income failed, and in 1846 when the potato crop failed thousands were left with no alternative but to migrate south or emigrate to the colonies. Between 1850 and 1950 the Highland population declined by at least 100,000.

Emigration

'Farewell to Glasgow,
Likewise to Lanarkshire,
And farewell my dearest parents,
For I'll never see you mair;
For the want of pocket money,
And for the want of cash,
Makes mony a bonny laddie,
To leave his bonny lass.'

Ballad c.1860

The main destinations of the emigrants were America - first to the Carolinas and New York and, after the American War of Independence, to Canada. From the 1840s emigrants began to favour Australia and New Zealand.

Wherever they went, the Highland emigrants carried their language, culture and traditions and transported to their new lands the place names of their homeland. In New Zealand 50% of the suburban names in Dunedin have a Scottish connection. In Canada there are nearly as many descendants of Scots as there are people living in Scotland; almost 5 million Canadians ticked the 'Scottish origin' box in the most recent Canadian census.

The Scottish Enlightenment

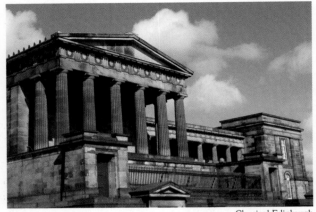

Classical Edinburgh

Although the story of the Highlands in the 18th and 19th centuries was grim, it was very different in the Lowlands. During the second half of the 18th century Scotland was in the forefront of intellectual and scientific developments. The movement known as the Scottish Enlightenment was concentrated on the university departments and laboratories of Edinburgh and Glasgow.

The intellectual leaders of this Scottish movement were the philosopher David Hume and the political economist Adam Smith. They had distinguished colleagues in scientific research. In 1756 Joseph Black, a lecturer in chemistry in Glasgow, published a paper demonstrating the existence of carbon dioxide. He also discovered the principle of latent heat and befriended the young James Watt, then working as a Glasgow laboratory technician.

In Edinburgh a 'Society of Gentleman in Scotland' was formed and between 1768 and 1771 produced the first edition of a dictionary of the arts and sciences entitled Encyclopaedia Britannica.

The confidence of Scotland during the Scottish Enlightenment is expressed in the magnificent New Town built to the north of medieval Edinburgh. Work began in 1767 and continued for half a century, with different architects all conforming to a style of restrained classicism and together creating a masterpiece of town planning.

The peak of elegance is Charlotte Square, designed by Robert Adam and named after George III's queen.

Industrial Scotland

Forth Rail Bridge opened in 1890

From the middle of the 18th century, Scotland was being transformed from a largely rural agricultural economy, to an industrial powerhouse. In 1831 half of Scotland's workforce was employed in agriculture but by 1891 this figure had shrunk to only one quarter of the working population.

Much of Scotland's new-found wealth rested upon the Atlantic trade, particularly in tobacco. Glasgow's famous Tobacco Lords were some of the great innovators of capitalism and accumulated vast sums of money.

Scotland had always had a coal industry and during the 19th century coal output continued to grow, reaching a peak in the early 20th century. Some of the expansion was fuelled by local inventions such as James Watt's steam engines which were used to pump water allowing deep mine shafts to be sunk to exploit coal and mineral reserves below Ayrshire and Lanarkshire.

During the same period Scotland developed a thriving iron industry. In 1830 the region had twenty-seven furnaces producing about 5% of Britain's output of pig iron. By 1860 there were 133 furnaces accounting for as much as 25% of national production.

In 1812 Henry Bell built 'The Comet', the world's first successful passenger steamship, which began the rise of the Clyde shipbuilding industry. In 1839 a Glasgow marine-engineer, Robert Napier, established the city's link with the Cunard company and was soon building iron ships both for Cunard and the rival P&O line.

The same steam engines were used to power the first locomotives and the railway industry. One of the major factors in Scotland's industrialisation was the development of a vast railway network which connected nearly every town in Scotland.

This rapid industrialisation led to the rise of great urban centres but also to massive overcrowding and slum conditions. At one point there were only five water closets in the whole of Dundee for a population of over 50,000. Disease and cholera epidemics were rife. The first cholera epidemic in 1832 killed 3000 in Glasgow alone. Concern about these conditions led later to huge improvements in town planning and civic responsibility.

Victorian Scotland

In 1842 the young Queen Victoria and her husband Prince Albert visited Scotland. She bought Balmoral Castle in 1848 and it has been the Scottish home of the British royal family ever since. In her journal Queen Victoria described Balmoral as "my dear paradise in the Highlands". After the death of Albert, Balmoral became a place of comfort for the Queen in the years that followed. So powerful was the special magic of the area that Queen Victoria, in the latter decades of the 19th century, spent as much as one third of the year at Balmoral. Much of this time was spent in the company of John Brown who had been Prince Albert's personal ghillie. The Queen commissioned a portrait of him and after his death she had a life-sized statue of him erected in the grounds of Balmoral Castle causing much scandal in the conservative Court.

Victoria's enthusiasm helped to make Scotland the fashionable place for wealthy Victorians to visit. In 1846 Thomas Cook organised the first tours of Scotland. The west coast railway line, running from Glasgow to Fort William and completed in 1894 at a cost of £700,000, opened up some of Scotland's most beautiful and dramatic countryside to visitors. Many of the visitors were rich who enjoyed shooting and other country sports.

Scottish oil

Like heavy industry elsewhere in Britain, Scottish shipbuilding and mining suffered a disastrous decline in the second half of the 20th century. At the same period Scotland acquired a new resource in the North Sea oilfields, which brought welcome new prosperity to regions from Aberdeen up to the vast terminal built at Sullom Voe in the Shetlands. However, it also brought much controversy about the way in which the revenues were spent, leading to the rise of Scottish nationalism.

Devolution

The Scottish Parliament building

The Scottish National Party won its first seat in parliament in 1945 but there was not much progress until the late 1960s, when nationalist returns at the polls first begin to make Westminster take notice. The surprise victory of Winifred Ewing in a by-election at Hamilton in 1967 was a turning point. A Royal Commission was set up to look into the constitutional aspects of devolution but it took another 30 years for the new Scottish assembly come into being. It was formally opened by Queen Elizabeth on 1 July 1999. The Scottish parliament resumed business in Edinburgh (though with powers limited to internal affairs) after an interval of 292 years.

Landscape

Geographically, Scotland is divided into three distinct areas: the Highlands, the Lowlands and the Islands. In terms of landscape, geology, history and culture they are very distinct. Scotland also has many of the UK's geographic extremes – the highest mountain, the deepest lake, the most northerly point and the most westerly.

Mainland Great Britain's most northerly point is not, as usually thought, John O'Groats but is actually the nearby Dunnett Head. Ask most people which is mainland Great Britain's westernmost point and they're likely to say Land's End in Cornwall, but they'd be wrong. It is actually Ardnamurchan Point, the tip of the peninsula that stretches between the islands of Mull to its south and Eigg, Rum and Skye to its north.

West Ardnamurchan is a wild, lonely, and stunningly beautiful place. The single track road is slow enough today, but until 1900 it could only be reached by boat. When you finally reach the point, ahead of you is Ardnamurchan Lighthouse. The lighthouse was built in 1849 with stone from Mull, one of 14 constructed in Scotland by the Stevenson family. Its particular claim to fame is that it is the only lighthouse in the world built in an Egyptian style. Even the keeper's cottages were influenced by the craze for all things Egyptian that swept Britain in the mid 1800s.

The road to Ardnamurchan lighthouse

Lowlands

Tide out on Solway Firth

This diverse region includes the most densely populated areas around Glasgow and Edinburgh as well as the wild Border country. This landscape bears the marks of its turbulent history with ruined abbeys and castles that were fought over for centuries. There is also the 10th century Traquair House which is said to be the oldest continually inhabited house in Scotland.

The region also boasts its own language, Lallans, or Lowland Scots, to distinguish it from the Gaelic of the Highlands and Islands. It was known as 'the Doric' or rustic language in contrast with the 'Attic' or 'Athenian' language of Edinburgh's literati, especially in the 18th century. The Scots Language website claims: 'Scots maun staun its ben as ane o three leids o the kintra, alang wi Gaelic an Inglis.'

Highlands

The Scottish Highlands have so much to offer – breathtaking mountains and lochs, romantic castles, handsome towns and villages and the wildest, least populated landscape in the UK.

Ben Nevis, Britain's highest mountain, rises dramatically from sea-level on the shores of Loch Linnhe, to tower 1,344m (4,406ft) above the town of Fort William. In Gaelic the mountain's name, Beinn Nibheis, means poisonous or terrible, suggesting its fearsome reputation. Its dramatic changes of weather, height and northerly location, make it a serious mountain not to be tackled lightly.

Loch Ness is the largest of three lochs located in the Great Glen which divides the North of Scotland along a line from Fort William to Inverness. The loch is large, 36k long and over 1k wide, and averages 200m in depth. It is most famous for the unstoppable stories of the Loch Ness monster.

The first recorded sighting of Nessie on land was made by Mr Spicer and his wife on July 22nd 1933. They were driving beside Loch Ness when they caught sight of a large cumbersome animal crossing the road ahead. They saw a long arched neck, a little thicker than a elephant's trunk, and a huge lumbering body heading towards the Loch. It disappeared into the bushes out of sight. After this sighting reports flooded in but despite much searching no conclusive proof has been found either way.

Munros

The brooding peak of Buchaille Etive Mor mountain in Glencoe

This is a list of all of the mountains higher than 3000 feet (now a less memorable 914m). The original list was compiled by the rather tragic figure of Sir Hector Munro. An early leader of mountaineering in Scotland he compiled the first catalogue of all of the hills above 3000ft and came up with a total of 280. He then set out to climb them all. He had climbed his second last one, a difficult scramble known as the inaccessible pinnacle on the Cuillin on the Isle of Skye, and intended to bag the final one in the summer of 1914. But he died on the Western Front before he could return.

The first person to complete all the Munros was the Reverend Archibald Eneas Robertson in 1901, who is said to have revealed the priorities in his life when he reached the final summit and kissed first the cairn and then his wife. His diaries have raised suspicions that he might have missed one of them out.

Until 1981, there were only 250 Munroists on record. But the total is now rising at the rate of 153 a year and now stands at around 2,200. The fastest circuit is 66 days, and one enthusiast finished his 10th round at the millennium.

The list of Munros changes regularly as surveying techniques improve and there are endless debates about summits and subsidiary peaks. In 1991, it was reported that a new Munro had been found and dozens of obsessives climbed it the next weekend - only to hear that the report had been wrong and the extra ascent had been in vain. The generally accepted number of Munros is now 284.

Islands

The harbour at Tobermory

There are hundreds of islands off the Scottish coast – mostly to the west and the north. Over 100 are inhabited with a total population of about 100,000. The biggest populations are in Lewis and Harris, while the smallest islands such as Lunga and Shuna have fewer than a dozen inhabitants.

The Northern Isles, Orkney and Shetland have cultural and historical ties with Scandinavia and the Vikings, whereas the west coast islands have more links with Ireland and the Celts. The southernmost of the Atlantic islands, Islay, lies within sight of the coast of Antrim. The Western Isles have the largest concentration of Gaelic speakers in Scotland.

The islands vary enormously in their landscape – Orkney has good pastureland whereas Shetland is barren and stony, so the Shetlanders rely more on the sea for their food. Arran is like Scotland in miniature, with the northern end mountainous like the Highlands and the south rolling like the Borders. Tiree is flat and windy but has the most hours of sunshine in the whole of Scotland.

Because most maps of Scotland include Shetland in a box near the top right hand corner, it is hard to get a sense of just how remote this group of islands is. They are nearer to Bergen in Sweden than Aberdeen and are further north than Moscow or southern Greenland.

Old Man of Storr, Isle of Skye

Culture

Some of Scotland's most potent symbols date back to her early turbulent history.

Saltire

In 832AD, a Pictish army under King Angus MacFergus, along with a force of Scots were fighting the Northumbrians for control of Lothian. The night before battle, Saint Andrew reportedly appeared to Angus in a vision. On the battlefield the next day, a saltire, or x-shaped cross, similar to the one on which Saint Andrew was crucified, appeared in the sky. This inspired the Picts and Scots and they defeated the Northumbrians who fled after their leader, Athelstan, was killed. The colours are supposed to represent the white of clouds and the azure colour of the sky. From that time, the Saltire became the national flag of the Scots.

The Scottish Saltire

Thistle

The prickly purple thistle was adopted as the emblem of Scotland during the reign of Alexander III (1249 -1286). Legend has it that an invading army led by King Haakon of Norway landed on the coast of Largs at night intending to surprise the Scots. In order to move more stealthily under the cover of darkness, the Norsemen removed their footwear. As they drew near the Scots, one of Haakon's men stood on a thistle and cried out in pain, alerting the sleeping clansmen. It was the Scots who won the subsequent battle.

Scottish thistles

Stone of Scone

The Stone of Destiny itself is a rather unremarkable block of sandstone, but it is hugely important to Scotland. The Stone was used for enthroning Scottish monarchs from around 400AD. It was reputed to 'groan aloud as with thunder' if anyone other than the legitimate heir to the throne sat upon it.

In 1292 John Balliol became the last king to use the Stone in Scotland as it was captured by Edward I in 1296 and taken to Westminster Abbey. Edward believed, mistakenly, that possession of the Stone gave him sovereignty over Scotland. It remained there for the next 700 years, a part of the throne of Edward the Confessor on which all new sovereigns sit during their coronation. The last time it was used was at the coronation of HM Elizabeth II in 1953.

On Christmas Day 1950 the Stone was taken from Westminster Abbey by a group of Scottish Nationalists and it disappeared for about four months. It was finally found in Arbroath Abbey and returned to Westminster. There is much speculation that a fake was substituted.

On St Andrews Day 1996, the Stone of Destiny officially returned north of the border and, amid much pomp and ceremony, was installed in Edinburgh Castle.

Clans and tartans

The Gaelic word 'clann' means 'children' or 'offspring' and includes the extended family of the tribal chief. The clan chief was a hereditary role inherited by the direct male descendants and was a powerful factor in Highland history. The chief protected the people and the land, and fought off enemies. The people provided their chief with food, cattle, rent, labour and military support. The strength of the clan as a military force was used to powerful effect by both sides during the Jacobite rebellions. After the battle of Culloden, the government was determined to crush all aspects of the Highlands which were thought to be a threat and this brought an end to the old system of clanship.

Each clan had its own tartan. The clans with brightly coloured tartans usually wore a darker one to go hunting. Each clan also had its own crest badge and motto - a short phrase often shouted in battle when the clan charged.

The original 'kilt' was a piece of tartan cloth, about two metres broad and four long, which was drawn round the waist and tightly buckled with a belt. The lower part came down to the knees while the upper part, the plaid, was drawn up over the left shoulder and used as a covering for the body in wet weather. It was a very practical garment for the Highlands providing both protection and allowing the wearer to wade rivers or ascend mountains with equal ease. It was suitable for the warrior, the hunter and the shepherd.

When tartans were outlawed in 1746, the Government or Black Watch pattern became the only legal one which was used by the regiments raised within Scotland. By the early 1800s, it was realised that the knowledge of tartans was being lost and this lead to efforts to preserve tartan designs. Tartans were reconstructed from portraits, collected on pilgrimages, demanded from clan chiefs and recovered from weaver's notes. Tartan became one of the most fashionable patterns in Victorian England.

Bagpipes

Different forms of bagpipe exist in many places around the world. The basic instrument is the same, a bag with a chanter and one or more drones. The bag provides a sustained tone while the musician takes a breath and allows several tones to be played at once.

The origins of the pipes in Scotland is uncertain but the Highlanders developed the instrument to its fullest extent and made it their national instrument. Clan pipers titles were mostly hereditary and held in much esteem.

There are two major types of bagpipe music. Cèol Mor big music - piobaireachd (pronounced pibroch) is the classical Highland tradition of theme and variations. Cèol beag - little music – is dance music, marches, strathspeys, reels, jigs and hornpipes. Lowland pipers played mainly songs and dance music.

In war, the penetrating notes of the pipes cut through the roar of battle and could be heard at distances up to 7km. Because of the importance of the bagpipes to any Highland army, they were classified as an instrument of war and banned after the defeat of Bonnie Prince Charlie in 1746.

Recently they have undergone a great revival and are now found in all walks of life. The pipes are also played all over the world, even in Oman where the Sultan has his own pipe band trained by Scottish pipers.

"Twelve highlanders and a bagpipe make a rebellion."

Traditional Scottish proverb

43

Castles

Eilean Donan Castle

Scotland has some of the most beautiful, romantic and awe inspiring castles – many witness to its turbulent history.

Dunvegan Castle on Skye is the home of the MacLeod chiefs. It is moated, its walls are 3m thick, it has dungeons and battlements and parts of it date from the 9th century. It has been continuously owned and occupied by the same family for nearly 800 years. It houses many treasures of the MacLeod clan including Rory Mor's two handed sword and the fairy flag believed to have been captured from the Saracens during a Crusade.

The oldest part of Blair Castle, the seat of the Duke of Atholl, dates from 1269 but the building has been extensively remodelled - all the turrets, towers and parapets were removed in the 18th century then restored in the Victorian era when the Scottish Baronial style became fashionable. The castle has been the site of much dramatic history. In 1745 Prince Charles Edward Stuart and the Jacobite troops rested there while on their way south and in the following year the structure was badly damaged during a bombardment to dislodge the Duke of Cumberland's English troops.

Brodick Castle, on the Isle of Arran, is linked with Robert the Bruce. Sir James Douglas stormed Brodick Castle at the beginning of the Bruce's campaign, and it was from Brodick that Bruce launched his liberation of the mainland, which seven years later was to lead to the Battle of Bannockburn in 1314.

Standing tall on its volcanic rock, 135m high, Edinburgh Castle dominates the city that has grown up around it. Much battered, besieged, repaired, rebuilt and extended over the past 900 years the castle has been the focus for Scottish national feelings. It was the seat of Scottish kings and at the heart of the building is the great hall with its wonderful hammer beam roof, built by James IV. It is now visited by about 1m people every year making it the most popular attraction in Scotland.

Highland Games

The origins of these games go back to contests of strength held among the clans in ancient times, a way for the chiefs and kings to choose the strongest men to serve as their warriors. During the Celtic revival of the early 19th century there was renewed interest in the traditions of the clans of the Scottish highlands and it was during the high Victorian period that the Highland Games began to come into their own as an attraction.

Over the summer months, there is now a packed calendar of Highland Games where people gather to watch participants from throughout Scotland and further afield. The most popular traditional events performed by the heavyweight athletes are throwing weights for distance and height, throwing the hammer and tossing the caber. In addition there is highland dancing, running, cycling, tug-o-war, solo piping, and pipe band contests with a large number of overseas bands taking part.

Each area's Highland Games has its own caber and the characteristics vary slightly. The Braemar caber weighs over 60kg and is about 6m long. The size, and particularly the length, of the caber means that enormous strength is required simply to balance it vertically, and even more is required to toss it. Contrary to popular belief, the caber is not thrown for distance but for style. The challenge is to heave the caber up so that its heavy end lands in the middle of the clock and the whole caber turns right over,

ending up with the narrow end pointing exactly towards
the 12 o'clock position.

Tossing the caber

Edinburgh

Although not originally the capital of Scotland, Edinburgh has always had a royal connection. King Malcolm III built his castle at Edinburgh, and his wife Queen Margaret built a chapel within its walls - now the oldest building in the city. Her son, David I built the Abbey at Holyrood, a mile to the East along The Royal Mile. Robert the Bruce granted Edinburgh a Royal Charter in 1329.

By the end of the 1500s it had become as the Capital of Scotland and the growing population built the high tenement buildings close to the Castle, most of which can be seen to this day. With the Union of Crowns in 1603, Edinburgh ceased to be home to the royal court.

After the Act of Union in 1707, Parliament also no longer met in Edinburgh, but the city prospered. During the Scottish Enlightenment new streets and thousands of houses were planned and built in the Classical style, making the city one of the most architecturally beautiful in the world.

Since the last war its prestige has risen not least because of the success of the Edinburgh Festival. In the 1960s the old city was being torn down and rebuilt at an alarming rate, but since then buildings have been restored using traditional and sympathetic methods. Now the city looks as though it will remain as one of Europe's most beautiful and historically interesting cities and it is once again home to a Scottish Parliament.

Glasgow

Glasgow City Chambers in George Square

Glasgow's rich and varied history stretches back almost two thousand years. Originally a small salmon-fishing village at a crossing point on the River Clyde, Glasgow has been shaped by war, trade and heavy industry to become a truly international city.

Founded by Christian missionary St Mungo, Glasgow became a major religious centre and the fine cathedral dates from the 12th century, although it has been extensively added to in the years which followed. In 1451 Glasgow University opened, the second in Scotland.

By the 18th century many merchants had acquired great wealth by importing sugar, rum and tobacco. They were known as the Tobacco Lords and built magnificent mansions in the city. However, life was very different for the city's poor who lived in crowded and unsanitary tenements.

The discovery and exploitation of vast deposits of coal and iron ore in the Glasgow area shaped the next two centuries of history as Glasgow powered the Scottish industrial revolution. 'Clyde built' became a watchword for quality and reliability for ships and locomotives.

The changing pattern of industry means that the Clyde no longer employs the vast numbers of workers in manufacturing but the city is re-inventing itself as a tourist attraction. It was named European City of Culture in 1990 and is now the third most popular tourist destination in the UK for overseas visitors behind London and Edinburgh.

Dundee

Dundee has been settled since prehistoric times, and Pictish earthworks and chambers can still be seen just beyond the city's boundaries. The city was an important trading port as long ago as the 12th century, and it was here that Robert the Bruce was proclaimed King of Scots in 1309.

Dundee is famous as the city of the three J's: Jute, Jam and Journalism. These three industries were the core of the city's commercial success. The jute mills in particular, from the early 19th century, were the foundation of the city's wealth. Profits from these were invested worldwide - the biggest cattle ranch in the USA was run from Dundee until 1951 and the Texas oil industry was largely financed by Dundee jute wealth.

The jam-making came about almost by accident, when a ship carrying a cargo of oranges was forced to put into Dundee harbour during a storm. A local grocer bought the oranges, which his wife then made into marmalade, and an industry was born.

Journalism is represented by DC Thomson who continue to produce newspapers, magazines and, most famously, the children's comics The Dandy and The Beano, launched in 1937 and 1938 and still going strong.

Perth

Known to the Romans as Bertha from the Celtic 'Aber The' meaning mouth of the Tay. The city has been a Royal Burgh since the 13th century and was a Royal residence throughout the middle ages. Nearby Scone is the ancient coronation site of Scottish monarchs.

The notorious Battle of the Inch was organised by Robert III in 1396. In an effort to end a long standing feud between the Kay and Chattan Clans, and to suppress wider trouble in the Highlands, the King arranged a fight to the death between 30 men of each clan. This took place in front of spectators, including the Royal Court on specially built stands. The battle started with each man firing three bolts from his crossbow, and the survivors then fought with daggers and axes. After a bloody afternoon, eleven of the Clan Chattan were still on their feet when the last survivor of the Kay contingent escaped by swimming across the Tay.

The Scottish Protestant Reformation began in Perth in 1559 when John Knox gave a sermon in St John's Kirk. There has been a church on this site in the centre of the city for at least a 1000 years.

Flooding by the River Tay has characterised the story of Perth right up to modern times. As recently as 1993 large parts of the town were inundated and many bridges have been swept away. The Tay, Scotland's longest river, is now more associated with salmon fishing and provides challenging sport.

Food and Drink

Haggis

Great Chieftan o' the Puddin-race!

It is not known when or where the haggis was first eaten. The most likely origin of the dish is from the days of the old Scottish cattle drovers. When the men left the highlands to drive their cattle to market, the women would prepare rations for them to eat during the long journey. They used ingredients that were readily available and packaged them in a sheep's stomach for easy transportation.

Lady Login's Receipt, 1856
Σ *1 cleaned sheep or lamb's stomach bag*
Σ *2lb dry oatmeal*
Σ *1lb chopped mutton suet*
Σ *1lb lamb's or deer's liver, boiled and minced*
Σ *1 pint stock*
Σ *the heart and lights of the sheep, boiled and minced*
Σ *1 large chopped onion*
Σ *½ teaspoon cayenne pepper, Jamaica pepper,*
  salt and pepper

Toast the oatmeal slowly until it is crisp, then mix all the ingredients (except the stomach bag) together, and add the stock. Fill the bag just over half full, press out the air and sew up securely. Have ready a large pot of boiling water, prick the haggis all over with a large needle so it does not burst and boil slowly for 4 to 5 hours. Serves 12.

Tattie-an'-Neeps or Clapshot

The traditional accompaniment to haggis
Σ 500g potatoes
Σ 500g neeps (swedes in UK, white turnips in US)
Σ 1 tablespoon butter or dripping
Σ 1 tablespoon chopped chives or 4 shallots
Σ salt and pepper

Cook the vegetables separately, drain and then mash them very well together, adding the butter or dripping and herbs. Season to taste and serve very hot.

Porridge

A form of porridge has been a staple of the Scottish diet since prehistoric times. Neolithic farmers cultivated oats along with other crops. 18th century cookbooks give recipes for 'Water Gruel' made of oatmeal and water, flavoured with butter and pepper. Porridge was easy to prepare as the grain only had to be cracked, not ground into flour, and was cooked very simply in a pot over a fire whereas bread required an oven.

Porridge formed a basis for many dishes: it was served with meat, stock or fat, as well as with vegetables, fruits, honey or spices. In older times a 'porridge drawer' in crofters' kitchen dressers was filled with fresh cooked porridge which was cut into squares when cold to take onto the hills for sustenance. Sugar only became widely available in the 18th century, so it was probably not used on porridge before then. Now porridge is widely recognised as a healthy food that is high in fibre and helps lower cholesterol.

Σ 115g oatmeal
Σ 150ml milk
Σ 600ml boiling water
Σ ½ teaspoon of salt

Mix oatmeal and milk together to form a paste, then add the boiling water. Heat and simmer for 15 minutes, stirring occasionally. Stir in salt and serve with milk.

Smoked salmon and avocado

Scotland is renowned for its salmon – both fresh and smoked.

Serves 4

Σ *250g smoked Scottish salmon, cut into strips*
Σ *4 slices of light rye bread*
Σ *Low fat margarine or butter (optional)*
Σ *1 avocado, thinly sliced*
Σ *150ml mayonnaise*
Σ *1 tablespoon chives, chopped*
Σ *1 tablespoon lemon juice*
Σ *1 red chilli, de-seeded and finely chopped (optional)*
Σ *salt and pepper*

On each slice of bread, spread the margarine or butter. Arrange a couple of slices of salmon and avocado on each slice. Mix the mayonnaise, chives, lemon juice, chilli (if using) and salt and pepper together and stand for 5 minutes. Pile on top of the avocado and serve immediately.

Salmon steaks with lime and ginger dressing

Serves 2
Σ *2 salmon steaks*
Σ *olive oil*
Σ *2 tablespoons vegetable oil*
Σ *2 tablespoons clear honey*
Σ *2cm piece of root ginger, peeled and finely grated*
Σ *salt and freshly ground black pepper*
Σ *juice and finely grated zest of a lime*
Σ *mixed green salad leaves*

Preheat grill to high. Brush the salmon steaks on both sides with olive oil and grill for 3-5 minutes on each side until cooked. Meanwhile, in a small bowl whisk together the vegetable oil, honey and ginger. Season with a little salt and freshly ground black pepper and add the lime juice and zest, mixing until smooth. Arrange the salad on two serving plates, top with the salmon and spoon the dressing over. Serve with buttered new potatoes.

Shortbread

A traditional Scottish teatime treat.

Serves 4

Σ 200g butter at room temperature
Σ 85g caster sugar plus extra for decoration
Σ 175g plain flour
Σ 60g ground rice

Preheat the oven to 150C or 300F or gas mark 2. Grease and line a baking tray. Beat the butter and sugar together until the mixture is light, fluffy and creamy using a wooden spoon or hand-mixer. Add the flour and ground rice to the bowl and, using a round bladed knife, mix it into a dough. Use your hands to form the dough into a ball. Flour a flat surface and place the dough on the surface. Form it into a round gently with a rolling pin turning the dough each time it is rolled. This will prevent it from shrinking while it bakes.

Place the round on the prepared tray and using the back of a spoon handle make slight indents all the way around the edge. Score the round into 8 segments using a sharp knife. Bake in the oven for 35-40 minutes. Leave to cook until it is slightly golden at the edge but still quite soft in the middle. Cut it into the segments straight away. Leave the shortbread to settle then after about 10 minutes sprinkle the top with sugar.

Dundee Cake

This rich, fruity cake became popular at the end of the 19th century. It is often served at Christmas.

Σ
- 170g butter
- Σ 140g caster sugar
- Σ 4 eggs
- Σ 225g plain flour
- Σ 40g mixed peel
- Σ 170g each of currants, raisins, sultanas
- Σ grated rind and juice of lemon
- Σ 1 level teaspoon baking powder
- Σ 2 tablespoons whisky
- Σ 30g split blanched almonds
- Σ 2 tablespoons milk mixed with 1 tablespoon sugar

Beat the butter and sugar until it is white and creamy. Add the eggs one at a time, with a spoonful of flour, beating well. Stir in the peel, dried fruit and lemon. Sift the flour with the baking powder and add to the mixture with the whisky. If it is too stiff, add a little milk. Place mixture in a 20cm greased and lined cake tin and flatten the top. Cover with foil or greaseproof paper and bake at 325F, 170C or gas mark 3 for two hours. Halfway through, take off the foil and arrange the split almonds in circles on the top of the cake. 5-10 minutes before it is cooked, brush the top with the sweetened milk to glaze. Keep in the tin for 15 minutes before turning out on a wire tray. Store in an airtight container.

Whisky

The original name for the spirits distilled in Scotland was *uisge beatha* - the water of life. Whisky production was driven underground by excessive taxation and by the 1820s, although almost 14,000 illicit stills were being confiscated every year, more than half the whisky consumed in Scotland was in effect 'duty free'. The situation was regularised in 1823 which enabled the whisky industry to develop into the huge international business it is now.

There are two basic kinds of Scotch whisky - malt whisky and grain whisky. Malt whisky is made from malted barley only, while grain whisky uses malted and unmalted barley plus other cereals. Malt whisky may be blended or kept as a single malt. The flavour of malt whiskies varies considerably according to the distillery, while grain whiskies may be made anywhere in Scotland.

The unblended single malts produce the finest, and most valuable, whisky. The most expensive in the world is the 1926 Macallan Fine and Rare Collection which was recently sold for £23,750 ($38,000) per bottle. It's now sold out!